M000286860

GHISLAINE
SENSATIONAL AND IMPURE

WILLIAM STEEL

GHISLAINE SENSATIONAL AND IMPURE

All Rights Reserved. Copyright © 2022 by William Steel. Printed and bound in the United States of America. All rights reserved. No part of this book may be reproduced or transmitted in any form or by any means, electronic or mechanical, including photocopying, recording, or by any information storage and retrieval systems - except by a reviewer who may quote brief passages in a review to be printed in a magazine, newspaper, broadcast, or on the internet - without prior written permission from the author.

For additional information, please contact the author directly at:

E-Post: William@WilliamSteelAuthor.com

For the most current information regarding book tour events, or to inquire about William Steel's availability for personal appearances and public speaking engagements, please contact:

E-Post: Press@WilliamSteelAuthor.com
Tel: +1 (934) 600-1140

Published by
STEEL THE SPOTLIGHT MEDIA

ISBN: 9780578343945

This book depicts the life experiences of William Steel, (a pen name that the author is using), as he remembers them. The conclusions expressed within these pages are matters of opinion and experience. Certain names may have been changed to protect the individuals' privacy rights.

Front and back cover art direction and graphic design by:
Anonymous

FOREWORD

AT THIS POINT IN HISTORY, ONE WOMAN, GHISLAINE MAXWELL, COULD DESTROY THE WORLD'S MOST POWERFUL MEN.

Dear Readers,

My name is Dr. Mary Bass. By way of education, professional training, and career experience, I am a forensic accountant, a senior level data scientist, and a fraud examiner. Although I understand that those titles sound *very* dull, I assure you that the work itself involves danger and risk – I do it all for the greater good.

More importantly, by way of life experience, I am a crime victim, a survivor *-so far, thankfully-* and above all else, I am a proud and relentless advocate for two severely underserved populations – crime victims and their surviving family members, and victims of wrongful incarceration in America.

Shortly after I finished reading William Steel's stellar debut novel, *Sex and the Serial Killer: My Bizarre Times with Robert Durst*, I mailed Mr. Steel a letter conveying my immense gratitude to him for his enduring bravery with confronting dangerous people who hold tremendous power and infinite wealth, as I recognize that the actions that Steel has taken, both in the real world and by virtue of publishing his written works, are nothing short of heroism. Steel's bravery is truly limitless. His compassion for humanity is boundless.

As a reader interested in learning exclusive details about the Ghislaine Maxell case, (and all the players surrounding her orbit during her lifetime thus far), you deserve to know the truth and the facts. All of them.

William Steel is by and large the most qualified insider to deliver the facts to you; by recounting his own experiences with Jeffrey Epstein and Ghislaine Maxwell.

In this first book in his series, *GHISLAINE SENSATIONAL AND IMPURE*, William Steel is fearless in his willingness to convey his personal vulnerability as a survivor of Epstein and Maxwell as well as fearless in his courageous feat of going public with what he has endured.

Steel calmly attributes his bravery in relation to his ordeals with Jeffrey Epstein and Ghislaine Maxwell to the many victims who have personally inspired him by coming forward themselves.

William Steel combines the personal and the literary. In the intensity and intimacy of his writing, William Steel reminds us that true crime narratives are *not* just stories - they are tragedies. These tragic stories must be told very publicly and loudly.

We will never advance as a society if the villains are allowed to victimize others under the cover of darkness, and with blind eyes turned by the gatekeepers and the protectors, and the victims living a silent nightmare, voiceless. Imagine if you were robbed of your voice, powerless, too terrified to speak.

Please help and support the voiceless, if you can. Please champion individuals like William Steel, who, while humbly going about his life, intervenes when he witnesses exploitation and victimization, and will lay down his life for anyone in need of help.

Thank you for your time and compassion, (*a million times over*).

Sincerely,

Dr. Mary Bass

'THE ONLY THING NECESSARY FOR THE TRIUMPH OF EVIL IS FOR GOOD MEN TO DO NOTHING.'

-EDMUND BURKE, 1729- 1797

CONTENTS

ACKNOWLEDGMENTS

First and foremost, I'd like to thank God for all of His love and wisdom in my life. For His incredible mercies that are indeed new every day. For His incredible protection during the years of darkness when I struggled with cocaine addiction and following my own crooked path. I am so grateful to now be in a position to be a zealous advocate for crime victims. That by virtue of my experiences, I'm able to now turn that back around and to help others.

My gratitude respect and undying love for my beautiful and highly intelligent fiancée, Dr. Mary Bass. She's not merely a Data Scientist, forensic accountant, and a respected Metaphysics scholar, she also shares my passion for crime victim advocacy, having both been crime victims ourselves. She also shares my passion for reaching back into the prisons to assist the wrongfully incarcerated their attorneys and loved ones, in any way we can. Thanks also to DiAnne, my future mother-in-law, for all of her love, support, and understanding, not just for me but for my jokes and even at, times my New York sarcasm.

Gratitude for the uber professional producers and crew of my new TV show for encouraging support at all times. For trying to make me look good and alert during grueling filming schedules. Stay tuned…

My appreciation and eternal gratitude to two dear friends also amongst my highly competent mentors, Gary Greenberg author of the groundbreaking tome, *The Beer Diet,* who also co-authored my first book with me.

Also, an extra special acknowledgement must be bestowed upon the ever-irrepressible Spin Man himself, former Vice President of NBC TV, founder and CEO of TransMedia Group Public Relations in Boca Raton, the preeminent, relentless, inveterate blogger, Tom Madden.

WILLIAM STEEL

INTRODUCTION

"The fact is that I can't unsee what I saw on those videos. I can't unhear Ghislaine's resounding demands for assistance in killing Jeffrey."
-*William Steel*

The primary subject of this book, Ghislaine Maxwell, is now infamous. She is currently on trial in New York City.

Ghislaine is facing criminal charges of Conspiracy to Entice Minors to Travel to Engage in Illegal Sex Acts, Enticement of a Minor to Travel to Engage in Illegal Sex Acts, Conspiracy to Transport Minors with Intent to Engage in Criminal Sexual Activity, Transportation of a Minor with Intent to Engage in Criminal Sexual Activity, and two counts of the crime of Perjury. (*View explosive actual Court documents in the Appendix*). Unless you have been living under a rock, no formal in-depth introduction is necessary.

Within the pages of this book, I disclose very detailed information about Ghislaine Maxwell and Jeffrey Epstein, from my own limited personal experience and knowledge of them both.

As you will discover during your journey of reading this book, I have previously made good faith efforts to bring Jeffrey Epstein and Ghislaine Maxwell, where I believe they belong, to justice.

In the interest of full disclosure, in my distant past I was trained as a locksmith, safe, vault, and alarm technician.
I applied and misappropriated those skills for many years to commit multiple high-end burglaries of jewelry, art, and collectibles across the United States.

Much of my judgment during this period of my life was admittedly poor given my painful struggle with cocaine addiction. Cocaine addiction takes an emotional toll on those suffering from the addiction, as well as on those around them. Addiction grows in a bed of emotional turmoil, and the feelings of anxiety, shame, guilt, powerlessness, and worthlessness that increase risk for addiction only become worse when chemical dependency deepens and takes over.

Cocaine abuse also creates fresh emotional complications for everyone that it affects, repeatedly.

Drug abuse manifests in a cyclical nature with multiple stages of addiction.

Recovering from my cocaine addiction used to seem impossible. I didn't think that I could marshal the toughness and discipline that I needed to interrupt and thwart the cycle of drug abuse that had controlled me for so long, but, with help from God, I did.

In my life, I will not be going backwards, only moving forward and moving on. The same holds true with this book, in which I am telling my true story, unburdening myself of the secrets of these dangerous demons, Jeffrey and Ghislaine, and I am moving forward.

My own short story is that I ultimately was incarcerated for many years for nonviolent offenses, culminating in a well-publicized prison escape in May of 2005 and a profile on the America's Most Wanted Website.

What only very few knew at the time was that in the years prior, I had escaped from prison several times and actually returned unnoticed.

The legal consequences for a series of crimes, primarily burglaries, grand thefts, and several incidents of fleeing from the police were so excessive and extreme that my Court sentences were often referred to as "draconian."

Sex offenders and even some murderers very often received far more lenient prison sentences then I had received.

One glaringly obvious example of injustice in the form of selective lenient sentencing is one of the subjects of this book, a prolific pedophile with an insatiable appetite for children, Jeffrey Epstein.

With approximately 40+ victims, Epstein was able to plead guilty and was allowed to serve his time in the Palm Beach County jail for approximately one year in a private wing of the jail which also allowed Epstein to leave the jail every day to go to his office, business, home, (*and to God only knows where else*), while he was supposedly serving a prison sentence that would have landed someone of lesser means, or of color, close to a life sentence for one count.

That the American criminal justice system is broken is a given. My upcoming book on the multidimensional subject of the American criminal justice system, and my own experiences of being in the matrix of the prison industrial complex will also include the opinions and suggestions of many.

Many people in political parties clearly have their opinions about the best way to proceed toward reform that they believe works and what they believe doesn't work, what holds down recidivism while simultaneously keeping the community safe. Evidence based best practices for starters.

After approximately two decades in prison, as it has been said, "*the days of darkness have certainly caused me to see the light*", definitely applies to me.

While incarcerated, early on I elected to steer clear of nearly everyone and all negativity. Unless someone was involved in positive activities or there was someone who needed my assistance, I kept to myself.

I stayed involved with various ministries, I took college and university classes, I worked for years in prison law libraries, and I served for years on the Offender Representative Committee.

This involved being a liaison between the other inmates and the administration. The program and position were essentially designed primarily to avoid potentially costly protracted litigation by being a mediator of sorts between the administration and offenders and bringing concerns from the offenders directly to the administration for hopefully, positive and prompt corrective action.

Aside from my other duties and in that capacity, I also worked as a liaison for the medical department, the dental department, the mental health department, and for the chaplain's office.

I decided several years ago while incarcerated to write a book about my life, sort of as a cautionary tale to help and to warn others.

With virtually no resources or assistance available to prisoners to get this done, I mostly kept very rough outlines accumulating over the years.

In a major case, I testified for the defense in Miami Federal Court regarding the innocence of a man wrongfully convicted and serving life for the murder of a Sheriff's Deputy that someone else had murdered.

Tim had a false confession beaten out of him by a corrupt and racist homicide Detective, who had a history of doing exactly that to extract false confessions to murders from others and mentally challenged blacks.

The real murderer was, in actuality, a jail detention Deputy as was concretely later proven by a stunning ATF investigation. A sting operation ensued upon the real killer during which he confessed. Innocent Tim Brown was freed from his life sentence.

Several years ago, I also had the misfortune of meeting an individual who was trying to frame another man for a murder he had committed. He detailed to me how he was framing an 18-year-old former acquaintance for murder in South Florida in Palm Beach County. Evidently, this scoundrel was offered a 15-year plea for his role in the murder, if he testified against this innocent party.

I contacted the innocent party's defense attorney and explained what I knew which, obviously, could have only been known by someone having a private conversation with the real murderer. The innocent party was Roy.

Roy did go to trial, and I was called as a defense witness. I testified about the plot that the real murderer had made to frame Roy.

My life was threatened by the real murderer because of my testimony, yet thankfully, the jury acquitted Roy and he was released and not sentenced to life.

During Roy's trial, the jury foreman was Gary Greenberg. Gary happened to be a true crime writer and editor at American Media International which, of course, includes The National Enquirer, The Globe, Star magazine and several other compelling publications.

After the trial, Gary and I connected and he began to encourage me in my writing, the telling of my story the story of my life, and with stories of some of the colorful, famous, and the many dangerous and despicable, and at times, infamous characters that I've met along the way.

During my lifetime thus far, I have had both positive and negative memorable encounters with masses of people that you, the reader, are almost certainly unacquainted with.

On the other hand, some of my encounters and adventures have transpired with people whom, likely, you have heard of. This is a condensed list; John DeLorean, Lisa Marie Presley, Robert Wagner, Dick Van Dyke, Sid Caesar, Dennis Farina, Andrew Dice Clay, and at one time one of the wealthiest men in the world and friend of the British Royal family- Krishna Maharaj, Jorgé Ayala aka "El Loco" cartel cocaine trafficker / assassin and one of the original Cocaine Cowboys, as well as Jack Hassan, the man behind the biggest diamond swindle in American history of approximately $80 million in diamonds.

I would be remiss if I neglected to mention genuine mafia Princess, author and journalist Susan Berman, and her now convicted murderer; the wealthiest serial killer in American history- Robert Durst, as well as Jeffrey Epstein and Ghislaine Maxwell. And I have literally not even begun to name drop.

Gary was and continues to be a mentor, encourager, and friend while I struggle with my writing. My style being "stream of consciousness", I'm told. Though I probably drove Gary crazy through almost a decade long period of my incarceration with my constant questions, phone calls, letters and requests, he hung in there with me, and then we decided to write a book together. My first book was to be purely about my life, and the characters merely footnotes in it.

However, one horrible human being from my past, Robert Durst, instead became the focus of my first book, *Sex and the Serial Killer My Bizarre Times with Robert Durst*, with Gary Greenberg as my coauthor.

I remain humbled that this my first book has received intense media coverage and was featured on the queen of true crime, Nancy Grace's podcast, *Crime Stories with Nancy Grace*. There is a lot of interest in getting this first book produced into a drama series or a feature film and I was working toward that end with Emmy nominated screenwriter extraordinaire, Bettina Gilois. Sadly, she passed away.

Around this time, a new mentor and friend came into my life. Tom Madden. Tom was the former Vice President of NBC TV in New York. Tom is now CEO of TransMedia Group Public Relations, a powerhouse that he Founded in 1981. TransMedia Group is likely the most effective and resourceful public relations firm on the planet, bar none.

Tom not only represented Gary and I in bringing publicity to our book, Tom also brought aboard a phenomenal attorney, Peter Ticktin Esquire, Founder of The Ticktin Law Group, to try to help me to get released early, as a non-violent offender, during this COVID-19 pandemic.

In my case, as a non-violent offender and with weeks to go on my sentence, it would seem like a no brainer to *not* let me die in prison while they were in the process of letting violent felons out of prison to clear space so that more people wouldn't die in prison. The horrific COVID-19 pandemic gripped the world, as Florida politicians and judges ignored my pleas for compassionate release a few weeks early while there was an outbreak going on at my prison, scores of people dead and dying.

Within months of my release, Tom Madden did another magnificent turn and introduced me to a woman who is now the love of my life and my fiancée, Dr. Mary Bass. We have a shared passion for assisting the wrongfully incarcerated, advocating for crime victims, and championing the underdog.

Within weeks of my release, I was offered and accepted a starring role on a docuseries / reality tv show on a major network that is focused on my life during my re-entry into society, post-incarceration. We have already filmed at least ten episodes. I'm advised by the network that this groundbreaking new series is set to air in the summer of 2022. Per my contract, I cannot yet discuss the name of the program nor the network it will be shown on.

I will say this - stay tuned! Now, almost a year out of prison, I spend most of my time writing books, toiling away at treatments and screenplays, attempting to get a foothold in public relations, and the most important and rewarding role of all is working side-by-side with my fiancée to zealously advocate, within the bounds of the law, for crime victims and the victims of wrongful incarceration. A few of those cases will be profiled briefly in the back of this book. More details are available on my website, williamsteelauthor.com

#DURSTurbed.

No, it's not misspelled. It was Tom Madden, *The Wordshine Man* himself, which is also the title of his next book, who created that word, "DURSTurbed", referring to the bizarre, sadistically murderous and psychotic world of the wealthiest serial killer in American history, Robert Durst. He is the twisted subject of my first book with coauthor Gary Greenberg, *Sex and the Serial Killer: My Bizarre Times with Robert Durst.* I have encountered other "DURSTurbed" people of his ilk, including Ghislaine Maxwell and Jeffrey Epstein, whom, though not accused nor convicted murderers, were in fact, twisted lovers, ringleaders intertwined in masterminding, (allegedly), a decades-long, demented, self-indulgent worldwide pedophilia organization, while simultaneously conducting clandestine blackmail operations of some of the wealthiest, most influential people on the planet. Maxwell and Epstein conspired to discreetly and frequently film themselves and their high-profile, powerful associates from around the world having sexual relations with very young girls.

This is the abbreviated story of how I came to know them.
And how I escaped with my life.

1 "G" AND ME

"Jeffrey is going to be the death of me", G said. *"I want you to kill him for me"*.

"G" was my nickname for the now infamous, Ghislaine Maxwell. It was what I called her then. With my Brooklyn ease and with the, to me, odd sounding pronunciation of her name, it was my quick and easy go to.

"Here we go again", I thought. Perplexed but not surprised given the faux dangerous persona I took care to cultivate around certain people, that G would want Jeffrey Epstein dead, but she was so self-absorbed and oblivious to what kind of person I *really* am that she would dare ask me to do such a thing. Others have asked to their eternal regret.

I was naked, drugged, restrained, and in excruciating pain.

Certain I was being filmed at my worst hour.

A wanted fugitive desperate to escape this Palm Beach mansion, desperate to flee as far as I could from G and her 30 something year-old lady friend whose name escapes me now. *Or does it?* But I digress.

Many years ago, I was professionally trained as a locksmith, alarm, safe and vault technician. A big fan of the original Mission Impossible TV series and James Bond movies. I wanted to emulate those guys. The guy who could get in and out of anything, the guy who could pull it off and all for the common good. To boldly vanquish evil in the world and to protect the vulnerable.

In my teens, I was one of the earliest members of the Guardian Angels, patrolling the most dangerous subway lines in New York City at a time when violent crime rates on the subways were skyrocketing.

The painful fact of my childhood was that my dear mother suffered with severe mental illness and was routinely picked on and bullied. I was her zealous defender. A role and life circumstance that ingrained in me a sense of doing what's right and standing up to bullies of every stripe, no matter the cost. Especially the scum that would dare to victimize women, children, the elderly or the mentally ill.

My heart was squarely in the right place.

I don't smoke, drink, use pills or smoke marijuana. Never did, never will. Yet after my best friend died in a terrible car accident, I was offered and then self-medicated the intense pain and grief with cocaine. Like so many others so afflicted, everything quickly changed.

I succeeded in a spectacular fashion to corrupt my skills and became a super thief of sorts.

A renowned and relentless connoisseur as it were, of millions of dollars in personally purloined ill-gotten gains: Artwork, jewels, collectibles of every sort. Lock-picking and circumventing alarms were my specialties. Nothing was out of reach. It was during this period and an unusual set of circumstances that I first met the now infamous convicted pedophile, and *alleged* prolific blackmailer, Jeffrey Epstein

2 MASTER OF THE PEDOPHILES

On world-renowned Worth Avenue in Palm Beach Florida, there are gorgeous palm tree lined sidewalks and there are many high-end and designer clothing and jewelry stores. Restaurants and elegant environs bustling with the super-rich and tourists. Its streets lined with ultra-luxury vehicles of every type. For years I've committed many crimes in and around Palm Beach and virtually all of South Florida not to mention coast to coast from Las Vegas to Los Angeles, Laguna Beach to Beverly Hills. Clean cut and playing the role of an affluent local, I was, many years ago, targeting waterfront and oceanfront communities, gated communities the intercostal waterfront communities, and the many mansions all throughout the area. Relieving them of their valuables, jewelry, collectables, and artwork.

I went out of my way to ingratiate myself with the locals, jewelers, homeowners, Realtors, and businesspeople, to keep my ears open for the next hit, the next potential target.

To a jewel thief, a *"Fence"* is someone who would knowingly buy stolen jewelry artwork, and collectables with no questions asked, no identification required or having to be shown, and one who understood the meaning of the word discretion. During my career as a jewel and art thief I had many such fences from Beverly Hills CA, in Laguna Beach CA, Las Vegas NV, and in New York City -

right in the heart of the diamond district. When it came to South Florida, I had many fences in Miami, particularly in the Seybold Building, a major hub of jewelers' exchanges.

Over the years in Palm Beach County Florida, I had several such reliable fences one of whom I will name - the notorious Jack Hassan; mastermind of an $80 million diamond swindle, the largest diamond swindle in history.

Another favorite of mine for very, very expensive jewelry was in Palm Beach itself, one of the wealthiest communities one of the most famous communities in the country.

Palm Beach was home to people like the Kennedy clan. The Kennedy family had a compound on Palm Beach for decades where President Kennedy lived. It was referred to as the southern White House. People like rock star Rod Stewart whose then wife Kate Hudson could be seen nude sunbathing on the beach. Even the Gucci family once had a gigantic house there. The list goes on. It was in this island of opulence that I had one of my most reliable fences. He owned a second-floor diamond salon that was only known to few. I was one of the chosen few, however, my business, as it were, was always nefarious.

I walked into the nondescript diamond dealer's salon. A place I've been to many times before, laden with stolen diamond encrusted jewelry to see my fence; or one of them.

Eager to quickly sell and leave, I was very disappointed to see that my fence was busy with a couple.

He seemed much older than the young girl he was with who appeared about 12 or 13 years old and a dead ringer, a doppelgänger for the Taxi Driver era Jodi Foster.

Pretending to think nothing of it, I feigned browsing while waiting to get the requisite privacy needed to haggle over my loot with my friendly fence. I'd imagine the guy thought I wasn't paying attention as I was perusing some jewelry displays at the other side of the salon. I looked back and noticed that, to my surprise, this older man had his hand deep inside of her shorts from behind. I faked a cough as if to let them know I was there or rather, to remind them that I was there, and he quickly pulled his hand out.

Then and there I made up my mind to confront him. Frankly, I was going to wring his neck right there, but my inclination was to immediately call the police.

However, I was right in the middle of many illegal activities, I had stolen jewelry with me, a pistol with a silencer on it with me, and my friend was the owner of the salon. A confrontation, assault, or a fight at this particular moment wouldn't be a good idea. I would wait to confront him outside.

Meanwhile, I would ask my friend, the owner of the jewelry salon, what his name was and where he was from. The likelihood was very high that he would tell me, and I would catch up with this stranger later that same day.

Once the girl and the man whom I now know to be Jeffrey Epstein exited the salon and walked downstairs, I told my friend that I had some jewelry for him to look at, but that I had forgotten a piece or two in the car and that I needed to go back down to my vehicle. The purpose of this was to give this guy about ½ a block head start so that I could see where they went, what vehicle he went into, maybe I could determine who he was, get a tag or a description of a car, or possibly strike up a conversation to determine who he was and who she was.

Quickly exiting back onto Worth Avenue, I looked up and down the block and I noticed the man and the girl walking up Worth Avenue towards the ocean and turning into a restaurant which, if memory serves me correctly, was called Ta-boó. When I arrived there just minutes behind them, I waited to confront him so as not to further traumatize the girl or bring attention to myself, considering all of the illegal things that I had on me.

They ordered and I ordered and when he eventually glanced over at me, I waved him over to me.

He arrogantly shrugged his shoulder like as if to say, "what do you want"?

So, I got up and quickly walked straight over to him at his table, put my hand on his shoulder, leaned into his ear and told him in a firm but quiet voice as possible, "I saw what you did in the jewelry store and it's in your best interest to give me one minute of your time so please step over to my table and sit down. I'm not going to ask you twice."

He came over and sat down grudgingly and had the nerve to ask me, "What can I do for you?".

I told him, "I'm Bill, what's your name?" After he told me I went on, "Like I said, I saw what you did in the jewelry store to that girl. She's gotta be underage. Who is she to you?". He said that she was his niece and that they always joke around like that.

I detected his Brooklyn accent, which is where I'm from, so I leaned into him and I said as firm as I could, "Listen motherfucker, I don't care if she is your niece, she looks like she's underage. What the fuck did you touch her like that for?".

He said, "She's not underage, she's 18".

"She sure as hell doesn't look like she's 18 to me", I said, "sit right here and if she doesn't tell me the same thing, you and I are gonna have a problem and if you get up from this chair before I finish speaking to her, we're going to have a problem".

I reminded him there are cameras everywhere,

numerous surveillance cameras in the jewelry store and what he did was caught on camera. Then I opened my bag and discreetly took out my gun and silencer right in front of him under the table- I screwed the silencer onto the gun- he started to get up I said, "sit down, you have no wins here". I chambered a round and stuck the gun in my jacket pocket. Then I walked over to the girl, sat down with her for a second, and introduced myself. I asked her for her name, and I asked how old she was and what was her relation to Jeffrey.

They must have had a rehearsed their story because her story tracked his. I told her, "OK I was just coming over here to make sure you were Ok". She said exactly what he had told me, "Yes I'm fine that's my uncle, he plays around like that". I knew the two of them were lying to me, but, as I said, I had a lot of illegal things with me; a gun, silencer, and the stolen jewelry was the least of it. I sat back down with him, and I said to him, "Jeffrey, you're both full of shit".

Before he had a chance to respond I asked him, "what part of Brooklyn are you from?". He recognized my accent to mean it and he immediately confirmed he was from Brooklyn. I believe he said he went to Lafayette High School while I went to Lincoln High School, and I grew up in the Gravesend / Bensonhurst section of Brooklyn. This Brooklyn "bond" of sorts allowed me to cut through the nonsense and his bullshit veneer of his purchased and blackmailed fake respectability...

I told him, and in no uncertain terms, that he better thank God I'm not a cop- and more importantly, he should be glad it wasn't her father walking up on him, "because if I was her father, I would have put a bullet in your fucking head." This particular, and now to the world disgustingly familiar character, that I met that day on Worth Avenue,

7

was in fact the now infamous, Super Villain like characters of the beloved James Bond movies, Jeffrey Epstein. A prolific pedophile hiding behind the veneer of an immensely wealthy educator, broker, socialite, and financier.

Fast forward to 2005, and the sweetheart 18-month deal in the county jail that he received after he had sex with approximately 40 minor young women in 2005, a deal *The Miami Herald,* in a series and now book of the same name by an extraordinary investigative journalist Julie K Brown termed a "Perversion of Justice."

Because the Victims' Rights Law requiring that the victims of this deal be notified was not followed, the victims' attorneys sought to address that.

This deal even covered complete immunity for all known and unknown co-conspirators, and it was drafted by the very attorneys that, in some cases, are suspected of being co-conspirators themselves. Meaning, that if this was the case, they crafted a deal for Jeffrey that, in essence gave them, including not just Jeffrey and Ghislaine, but anyone else involved with these crimes of trafficking sex with minors in the Southern District of Florida, complete immunity, forever, from any prosecution there.

However, what these genius attorneys didn't stop to consider was that it was not a global deal encompassing all Federal and State Districts and jurisdictions.

So much outrage was then generated that the FBI and U.S. Attorney's office in New York City conducted a phenomenal investigation, not plagued by the massive leaks which were the hallmark of the Florida ones, and subsequently arrested Jeffrey again in July of 2019 for the sex trafficking of minors in New York. Jeffrey was now, by secret sealed grand jury indictment, charged in the Southern District of New York with:

Count 1: Sex Trafficking Conspiracy

Count 2: Sex Trafficking

Deemed an extreme flight risk he was denied bond.

He was held in the Federal jail MCC in Manhattan and just over one month was found dead in his cell. Hanging.

All the videos that could possibly cover this incident, all camera recordings mysteriously disappeared. No investigator could locate them, and no media could locate them. Epstein was supposed to be on a sort of suicide watch, mandatory to have a cellmate because it was suspected that he attempted suicide a few days before. Whether or not that was the case, or another inmate tried to kill him, is up for debate. However, their own institutional policies were violated by not having a cellmate with him. Furthermore, the officers that were supposed to be watching him and who were supposed to both be performing checks every 15 minutes on all the prisoners in that unit were instead taking turns sleeping on the job and using the Internet. Which they have now been convicted for.

The inexcusable gross dereliction of these officers sworn duty, and abysmal jail conditions, directly led to Jeffrey's death and the re-victimization of Jeffreys many victims who now forever lost the opportunity to confront him in court.

With all of the people that Jeffrey Epstein and Ghislaine Maxwell have blackmail evidence against, they can easily not only blackmail them for cash, for deals, for favors, even for favors within the judicial system, that same evidence can be used to destroy the careers of politicians, celebrities, and powerful people all over the world. Including Royalty. Some of these people are Arab Princes, some of these people are connected to intelligence agencies, literally the most powerful people in the world.

Epstein's death was ruled a suicide. Certainly, an arrogant coward like Jeffrey who destroyed the lives of young girls for his own sexual gratification and to pass around as pawns in the blackmail scheme was surely capable of suicide. However, there is much evidence that points to murder instead, as murder would just as effectively silence him forever.

Allegedly, it is rumored and whispered that many of these compromising blackmail videos had the likes of former United States President Bill Clinton, Harvard Law constitutional law professor Alan Dershowitz, Prince Andrew Duke of York from the United Kingdom, actor Kevin Spacey, Harvey Weinstein, as well as dignitaries from Canada, The United Kingdom, Australia, and Japan included.

During my many visits to the house on El Brillo Way in Palm Beach, Florida, to which I would mostly go when I had an interesting piece of jewelry to sell for some quick cash from Jeffrey or Ghislaine, I saw some of these videos.

They certainly didn't need to buy stolen jewelry from me. But they had a steady stream of people that they told me were "models" and "masseuses" in and out of the house and assured me that the jewelry items were gifts for them.

The house had nude photographs and art depicting young women in virtually every room. When I told Jeffrey point blank, "it looks like you have a lot of illegal photos here", he said the women in them were not underage and if they were, he's untouchable to the police. I never did see in person or participate in any sexual activity with any minor in that household.

I was asked specifically from both Jeffrey and Ghislaine to look for and ask any young woman that I know that might want to earn a few dollars to come to the house with me to be introduced to Ghislaine so she could prepare and train the girl to give massages to Jeffrey. Never did I fulfill that request. I pretended many times that I was on the lookout just to stay in their good graces and keep the money train coming for the stolen jewelry. But I never knew if they were serious, and I didn't want to be around if they were.

There came a point where Ghislaine and I became intimate. On several occasions.

At one point, Jeffrey came standing naked at the doorway as if he wanted to walk into the room and join in.

I yelled and warned at him and no uncertain terms to get lost. Ghislaine tried to convince me to get him to join in. I told her to shut the fuck up and don't even go there with me because it's not happening. After that incident I warned her that if he ever tried to invite himself into bed with me again that I would kill him.

She asked me if I was interested in any of the models that I saw. I told her in no uncertain terms, "no!" They had already told me that the entire house had cameras, the majority of which I never saw, even with my experience at looking for security devices. I suspected then and now, in hindsight, and rightfully so, that they were also trying to get me on film doing something illegal or embarrassing to then later use against me. As it now turns out, they've done exactly that to virtually everyone they've ever met.

I was astounded that these two were one in the same and that she would constantly attempt and actually find young girls for Jeffrey to molest, rape and film. More so considering he once told me that Ghislaine was to him, "a useful idiot."

Not long after I told Ghislaine that I would kill Jeffrey if he joined us in bed, I found myself in bed with her again along with an adult female companion /assistant of theirs.

Jeffrey had the nerve to appear at the bedroom door in a bathrobe, this time accompanied by another man. A rather large, powerfully built man with what looked like a semi-automatic pistol of some kind in a holster over his shoulder. His presence and his standing, leaning on the door jamb, was clearly to intimidate me and keep me trapped in the room. Likely one of his security detail or personal bodyguard. Don't forget the very first day I met Jeffrey, I confronted him about the young girl and pulled a gun on him. Then just before this incident I warned Ghislaine that I would kill him. He was evidently biding his time to get back at me. Carefully, Jeffrey ordered Ghislaine out of the bed and handed her a stack of compact discs. He told her to play them for me one at a time.

As I've said previously, there are some things in life you can go through your entire life wishing you had never seen and there are some things in life that you see that, unfortunately, cannot be unseen.

3 THE ROYAL SCEPTRE

The very first video I saw was with a clearly very young underage female having sex with Prince Andrew, Duke of York, from the United Kingdom. The man who would be King, a long shot, but possible. At first to me he was somewhat recognizable, but I did not realize who he was in his plain clothes and I'm not a big fan nor follower of the Royals.

I tried to get out of bed, and I told Jeffrey, "I don't need to see this. I don't want to see this."

"I'm not into adults taking advantage of kids", I said to him very sarcastically. As I tried to get up, Sarah grabbed my hand and pulled me back into the bed while a man with a rather large and intimidating frame standing at the door simultaneously said, "don't get up." Ghislaine looked frantic and grief stricken and turned beet red shaking her head slowly while looking at Jeffrey and then back to me.

Jeffrey comforted her by telling her, "There's nothing to worry about. Bill knows what will happen to him if he says anything about it when he leaves here."

A feeling of complete helplessness and terror swept over me. My tough guy façade quickly faded when I realized I was in way over my head. These people were truly dangerous. Truly, they had a lot to protect, and Jeffrey's countenance had changed so dramatically, so completely, that all I saw was pure evil that day. To see

13

someone who, as far as I knew, could possibly one day become the King of England with a girl so young doing everything imaginable, (which I won't describe in this book), caused me to hyperventilate. My life would have been just fine never having seen that. Never having heard him and the girl joking as they spoke of his privates as the "Royal sceptre."

I began to literally get chest pains because I had also been using cocaine earlier that day as well. As this particular first DVD played, it was clear that it was a composite of Prince Andrew being filmed having sex with minors at various locations on different occasions, including outdoors, poolside. At no time did he seem to be aware of the cameras, so I presume they were hidden.

Though I was terrified, I did try not to show it. I sarcastically said to Jeffrey something like, "so that's literally Prince Andrew, Queen Elizabeth's son?".

Jeffrey then had a gleeful smile on his face he said, "yes, it is. He is like my Super Bowl trophy, and I own him, and he knows it." I closed my eyes for the majority of this and vividly remember one young girl uncomfortably repeating the name she was told to use for Prince Andrew's private parts.

As they played other videos, I saw both Ghislaine and Jeffrey having sex with clearly underage young women. *Girls,* really.

In practically every instance, this would start with a massage for Jeffrey. Ghislaine stood by either nude or disrobing, and they were undressing the young woman.

It's like the two of them were kids in a candy store, only the "candy" for them was these underage girls.

In more than one case, Ghislaine named the girl and spoke about which one was her favorite and which one she found for Jeffrey.

I was trying to figure out who these girls were to see if I could provide more detail to the police and the police would be able to reach out to them, or maybe serve a warrant on the house and seize some of this material. But they never went into that kind of detail, other than the occasional first name of the girls.

One girl, particularly young in appearance, seemed to be about 13, was blonde with blue eyes. Jeffrey was mesmerized, staring at the screen, and said to Ghislaine, "that's one of the best ones you ever got for me. She gives one of the best blow jobs I ever had".

Ghislaine made it very clear on more than one occasion that she had to teach these girls how to give "proper blow jobs", as she referred to it. She claimed that she had to teach them this because only a certain technique would please Jeffrey, who had an insatiable sexual appetite, she said.

Other quite uncomfortable videos that, again, looked like the individuals did not know that they were being filmed, were of a very recognizable Bill Gates, Harvard constitutional law professor Alan Dershowitz, and billionaire founder of Victoria's Secret lingerie Les Wexner.

Though I didn't recognize him at the time, I'll never forget Jeffrey telling me who the guy was and then years later seeing him in media accounts tied directly to Jeffrey.

Other videos had in them, not surprisingly, serial kinky philanderer Bill Clinton, and for me, not surprisingly Hillary Clinton.

Was it clear whether or not there was a very well-known Australian celebrity as well? Or John Travolta, Kevin Spacey, and Harvey Weinstein? Michael Jackson, oddly enough? It was. There was even black and white footage of a very young Rolling Stone front man Mick Jagger, with another man and Prince Margaret.

To be clear, Mick Jagger was not with a minor. Ghislaine told me the woman was Prince Margaret and then, at my observation, she was clearly an adult at the time.

4 "MUMMY, I EXIST!"

Although early tragedy seemed to envelope Ghislaine Maxwell's life, this in no way excuses her reprehensible behavior as an adult. A highly educated and worldly woman coming from magnificent wealth, an international socialite, media heir, immersed in upper-crust society and with seemingly endless connections to the global superclass. Ghislaine didn't just casually name-drop her connections or boast about elites whom she didn't know, she and Jeffrey, actually knew them and knew them intimately, in many cases. Her personal relationships and close friendships with the members of the British Royal family, heads of state and ambassadors from around the world, a plethora of celebrities, entertainers, rock stars, as well as her personal involvement with international millionaires and billionaires have all been established as fact. All very well-documented by countless news outlets, first-person accounts, and on social media.

Virtually every one of these high-powered and influential connections Ghislaine and Jeffrey Epstein allegedly came to later manipulate and to exploit. Even to blackmail.

In 1961, Ghislaine's older brother, Michael, was crushed in a tragic car accident just days after Ghislaine's birth. He languished in a coma until his death in 1967. According to family insiders, Ghislaine was mostly, in this trauma- consumed family period, ignored during these early years while all attention was focused on her brother Michael and his coma. When suddenly, she, in frustration, confronted her parents in exasperation emphatically stating, "Mummy, I exist!". Things in in the Maxwell household irreparably changed from that day forward, it seemed.

Evidently guilt-ridden, Ghislaine's parents and particularly, her otherwise tyrannical father then began to shower her in every conceivable way with all the attention they've been inadvertently withholding from her during the years while in the midst of the deep family trauma of Michael's coma and passing. This included spoiling Ghislaine with all manner of materialism and opulence.

In 1986, her father, Robert Maxwell, media tycoon and scoundrel, purchased a 180-foot super-yacht which he christened *Lady Ghislaine*.

Thereafter, and by Ghislaine's own account, she quickly learned the art of manipulation and how to get exactly what she wanted from her tycoon father, and slowly but surely, from all of those around her.

After getting to know her, she eventually opened up about just exactly how she came to become the darling of her father's eye, despite having many other siblings.

She explained that her father would treat her more like a wife than a daughter. Including, according to her, sexually.

Ghislaine explained that she and her father

5 ROBERT MAXWELL

Ghislaine's father, Robert Maxwell, was a media baron, tycoon, titan, and tyrant. He was born Jan Lidvik Hyman Binyamin Hoch on June 10th, 1923, into abject poverty in Czechoslovakia. He fled Nazi occupation and ultimately ended up settling in France. Once France fell to the Nazis, Robert Maxwell found himself in Great Britain. He began a new life in a new country with a new name. In 1945 he married Elisabeth. Together they had nine children, including Ghislaine.

Robert Maxwell went into business becoming a distributor for a publisher of scientific books. He later purchased an interest in a small publisher and eventually he and his partners changed the name of the company to Pergamon Press. Soon thereafter, it was built into a major publishing house. Representing the Labour Party, Robert Maxwell was then elected as a member of Parliament for Buckingham and then re-elected a few years later.

Early on, Robert Maxwell was suspected of being involved with multiple frauds. He was accused of falsely stating that a subsidiary responsible for publishing

20

encyclopedias was extremely profitable.

It was later proven that Maxwell did in fact contrive to falsely inflate Pergamon's price by way of transactions between multiple family companies.

Although scandals seemed to follow him, the tyrannical Robert Maxwell managed to become a media tycoon. In the mid-80s, he acquired The Mirror Group newspapers. Mirror Group published six newspapers in the United Kingdom including The Scottish Daily Record, Scottish Sunday Mail, Sunday People, The Sunday Mirror, and The Daily Mirror.

Even employees referred to him during this period as a crook and a liar. In the latter part of the 1980s, Robert Maxwell also acquired Maxwell Directories, Prentice Hall Information Services, Berlitz language schools, Nimbus records, and part of MTV in Europe and many other European television services, including Maxwell Cable TV and Maxwell Entertainment. At one point, he purchased The European. Robert Maxwell also famously bought the New York Daily News.

Robert Maxwell also had numerous well-known ties to the state of Israel. Including, it is rumored, Maxwell providing covert help smuggling aircraft parts into Israel that led to air superiority during Israel's 1948 war of independence.

Furthermore, it was whispered and cryptically acknowledged by no other than Israeli Prime Minister Yitzhak Shamir during Maxwell's eulogy stating that Robert Maxwell, "has done more for Israel than can today be told."

Additionally, at least six serving and former heads of Israeli intelligence services attended Robert Maxwell's funeral in Israel.

The Foreign Office long suspected that he was a secret

agent of a foreign government.

He was more than likely a double or triple agent. Aside from this, it is claimed that Robert Maxwell was a thoroughly bad character and almost certainly funded by Russia.

Maxwell's links to the Soviet KGB, the British Secret Intelligence Service (MI6), and to the Israeli intelligence service Mossad have been well-established.

The only personal information I have about any of this is from Ghislaine. When I discuss my personal experiences within this book, I make it clear that that is exactly the case. For the purposes of clarity and context only, I conducted some minor research.

In early November 1991, Robert Maxwell's naked body was found floating of the Canary Islands.

It is assumed that he fell off the *Lady Ghislaine* accidentally while in the midst of a heart attack and then drowned.

Ghislaine however, was convinced her father was murdered. He had accumulated many, many enemies.

Despite this fact, he was buried on the Mount of Olives in Jerusalem. Robert Maxwell, the media titan, intelligence operative, and swindler, had a funeral attended by no less than the Israeli president, the Israeli Prime Minister, many foreign dignitaries, and politicians, and at least six serving and former heads of Israeli intelligence.

It was discovered that he looted hundreds of millions of pounds from his various companies' pension funds to shore up The Mirror Group shares and to save his own companies from bankruptcy.

It wasn't until many years after his death that in 2007 it was discovered that Robert Maxwell had in fact bugged the officers and recorded the conversations of many of his employees

Is it possible the lessons of recording one's real or imagined enemies or anyone within your orbit on video to blackmail them, a technique utilized by many countries' intelligence agencies worldwide, was not lost on Robert Maxwell, Ghislaine or upon Jeffrey Epstein?

It does seem that while Jeffrey and Ghislaine were plugged into countless powerful influential and governmental people worldwide. This is including royalty and world leaders. That is a fact that was so immediately demonstrable, that it was certainly personally and financially immensely beneficial to them to not only network, but to have dirt on so many people who, like them, are pedophiles. Beneficial if only they could look themselves in the mirror, that is.

6 ELISABETH MAXWELL

Ghislaine's mother was Elisabeth, and she was born in 1932, later marrying publishing tycoon Robert Maxwell in 1945. She had nine children, two of whom died in childhood. She received many awards in her lifetime and was a proponent of interfaith dialogue. Elisabeth even studied law at the Sorbonne. She also did public relations work for her husband Robert, and in spite of Robert's many shortcomings, crimes, frauds, controlling behavior, and evident abuse of Ghislaine, she supported and loved him, nonetheless. She's often been described as a wonderful, kind, and supportive woman. Which is demonstrated by her activities as a stellar and compassionate Holocaust researcher. After Robert's death in 1991, Elisabeth was left essentially destitute when it was discovered, and evidence emerged that Robert Maxwell had been looting his company's pension funds. She still maintained her dignity and lived her life mostly with family members and helping others.

My personal observation and opinion is Ghislaine would have been far better served to emulate her wonderful mother and follow in her footsteps, instead of utilizing her social standing, wealth, and connections to satiate her own and Jeffrey's mutual deviant sexual appetites by victimizing young girls in assembly line like fashion worldwide.

Certainly, Ghislaine will portray herself as a victim. And yes, perhaps she was a victim of her father's abuse she described very clearly some of the things she learned from her father, and not all of them good.

Instead, Ghislaine was fulfilling her debased desires for money, false accolades, and the approval of her perverted puppeteer in crime, Jeffrey Epstein. She is no victim.

As an adult, Ghislaine is a victimizer. She went out of her way as a woman to betray young girls, from what I understand young girls for mostly desperate circumstances, gain their trust, pretending to be their friend, pretending to care about them, their careers, their dreams, their family members and their personal and medical problems.

Ghislaine would desensitize these girls to sexual matters, portraying nudity as normalcy in front of them, personally teaching them how to give sexualized massages to Jeffrey, (and God knows who else), teaching these young girls the correct way to give Jeffrey oral sex.

Then Ghislaine succeeded in keeping them terrified and trapped by reminding them, and me, and others, of who she and Jeffrey knew, and what would happen to anybody who went to authorities.

In my case, it's well-documented that I came forward a few times, was essentially ignored and in all actuality, I didn't push the matter because I too lived in terror while Jeffrey was still alive.

It's no less concerning now what would happen, how many more people would die under very mysterious circumstances by experts in the art of death if and when some of the actual videos which I saw, and some of which the FBI most likely has from Jeffrey's New York home, ever came to light.

25

My nightmares come from the memories of seeing with my own eyes Ghislaine and Jeffrey did to so many young girls. And how Ghislaine would serve them up on a silver platter to Jeffrey, and any one of his associates who was up for the experience.

To me and any normal, civilized person with children, they should appropriately be viewed with most contempt and scorn, and it is my hope that the brave victims who have come forward publicly and the ones that are still too embarrassed or terrified to come forward but are speaking privately, will one day find peace and healing for what these monsters did to them.

I commend them all as well as the victims' rights attorneys that have represented them over these past few years.

An incredible job by a renowned Private Investigator deserves mention.

In the Palm Beach County state case, despite there being 35 to 40 victims and a prepared 53-page indictment for federal charges, Jeffrey was allowed to plead to solicitation of prostitution.

And I ask in what universe do you label a 14-year-old girl a prostitute?

For this single count he was sentenced to 18 months in the Palm Beach County jail stockade, in a private wing of the jails relaxed, minimum custody stockade, and of that 18 month, he served only 13 and was allowed to leave the facility for 12 hours a day six days a week. Ever the manipulator, he was seen not just using his bizarre authorization for work release to go to work at his office, he was spotted going to his house he was spotted going to his helicopter no one knows with any certainty, where he went.

After this joke of an incarceration in the Palm Beach County jail private wing. A wing in which his cell door was never even locked, and he was allowed special food.

He was then sent to supposedly go home and submit to a period of house arrest with very strict conditions.

One of the most phenomenal, tenacious victims' rights attorneys on this case, Brad Edwards who zealously advocated for the victims and even had Jeffrey Epstein squirming in his chair during deposition with very, very probing questions that he, a malignant narcissist like Jeffrey, could barely tolerate and had him writhing out of his chair.

Also, attorney Brad Edwards previously brought in and continued using excellent, dogged, private investigator, Mike Fiston.

Fiston was a 30-year Miami homicide detective turned Private eye who was responsible for recovering Epstein's black book during an FBI sting. He confirms that Bill Clinton traveled upon Epstein's private jet, coined "the Lolita Express" twenty-two times, and on all occasions the flight attendants were underage girls dressed as candy stripers. Fiston not only located about 46 more victims than were previously known, he also followed Jeffrey around during the farcical house arrest.

Jeffrey was supposed to be staying in his beautiful mansion on El Brillo Way in Palm Beach. Instead, the private investigator was able to follow Jeffrey going to New York, to his helicopter, to his airplane, to Miami and many, many other places while keeping a very thorough log of these violations of his house arrest/probation terms that, under Florida law, are themselves a violation of law, each and every time he violated his house arrest.

When Private Investigator Mike Fiston contacted the very people that were supposed to be supervising the house arrest, he claims he was told, "Well, what we what can we do about it, there's nothing we can do, he's a celebrity."

If somebody that was supposed to be supervising a prolific pedophile of hundreds if not thousands of young girls can be termed a *"celebrity"*, there's something wrong in this matter and far beyond what anybody has ever been told about this man and about this case.

Investigator Mike Fiston deserves, in my opinion, some kind of award for his tenacity and results. His investigations, in conjunction with the initial Victims' Rights Attorneys, under normal circumstances, would have resulted in the subject of his investigations ending up in prison for many life sentences. Not so with the seemingly Teflon Jeffrey Epstein. John Gotti, rest his soul, has got nothing on him.

Other tenacious individuals involved with victim advocacy were victims' rights attorneys Spencer Kuvin, Melissa Bloom, David Boise, Gloria Allred, and many more incredibly dedicated and compassionate attorneys.

A few years ago, when I attempted report some of these events yet again, one of these victims' rights attorneys and I established brief contact with, and that I agreed to assist him, if it would assist the victims and law enforcement and gathering any other additional evidence or information about Ghislaine Maxwell or Jeffrey Epstein, and other members of their staff, that were completely complicit in the commission of these horrific crimes.

There wasn't much follow up. I don't know the reason why it may be perhaps because the victims' compensation fund was beginning to pay compensation victims, or this attorney, perhaps, felt that I was not needed.

Perhaps not credible enough, although, we never had an in-depth conversation about my information to reach any such conclusion.

Pretty much, when I brought these matters up again and explained what had happened to me, I was in counseling. I felt it wasn't taken very seriously at that time either. The feeling I had was that nothing could be done because I wasn't underage at the time and these incidents started off as consensual between Ghislaine and I. And the incident where I was restrained and abused by Ghislaine, and her assistant, most likely had a statute of limitations where I could not prosecute, even if I wanted to.

Prosecution of these people wasn't my intention of bringing this up in counseling. My intention was to simply receive counseling and to try to somehow, come to terms with what had happened to me and to perhaps assist the other victims in any way that I could.

Additionally, whoever came up with the bright idea to prosecute Jeffrey and Ghislaine in New York, outside of the jurisdiction of the Southern District of Florida where they receive blanket immunity; to that person or persons, whether it be victims' attorneys, federal agents, or prosecutors, bravo on that strategy. Some of Jeffrey's attorneys at that time were long suspected of being amongst the very coconspirators, all known and unknown, that were given blanket immunity as a condition of Jeffrey Epstein's original, disgusting, and disgraceful plea deal in Palm Beach County, Florida.

No one cares if Jeffrey Epstein was working with intelligence agencies and that the disgusting blackmailing of dignitaries with videos of sex with minors is an "acceptable" technique in certain countries' spy circles.

No matter what intelligence value that Jeffrey Epstein was allegedly acquiring in complete partnership with Ghislaine Maxwell, it simply does not excuse the inexcusable, and the sexual exploitation of anyone in this world, and particularly the robbing of the innocence of children, is deplorable and impossible to justify.

In all societies, particularly an allegedly civilized society like the United States of America, where, supposedly, the rule of law and respect for the rights of others are upheld as inalienable rights, where we are taught to respect and protect women, children, the mentally ill, the elderly, the weak, the marginalized, and the vulnerable, we should have the basic moral decency to look out for them, the common sense, and the humanity to get involved and to help those in danger, those in need.

7 FAÇADE

"All the world's a stage,
And all the men and women in it merely
players;
They have their exits and their entrances.
And one man in his time plays many parts."

- William Shakespeare

Everyone, absolutely everyone, without exception, and especially each character in this melodrama, does indeed play a role. Some, chameleon-like, play whatever role is needed to acquire what they want. Others stay in clearly defined lanes, rarely deviating.

As I struggled with a severe cocaine addiction many years ago, I too played many roles as a matter of survival mostly. And many times, to acquire what I needed or wanted. During this period, I also invented many roles.

When dealing with dangerously treacherous people like Robert Durst, Jeffrey Epstein, and a few others, I would assume the role of a shrewdly connected - even dangerous man who was not to be toyed with.

Aside from being extremely well dressed, I would routinely have guns on my person, in my briefcase and / or around me. Normally on me, at least one handgun with a silencer on it.

Opening a briefcase in front of a fence to take out a package containing thousands of dollars in high end jewelry, or a few kilos of coke, seeing a gun with a silencer on it sent, in those years, a powerful message to the fence or shady associate not to screw with me. That very message was sent loud and clear to Jeffrey on day one. What I certainly didn't know at that early stage then was that he was clearly many, many times more dangerous than I could ever have imagined.

That Jeffrey and Ghislaine ran a gigantic international sex trafficking ring of young girls, that he had every inch of his homes and aircraft wired for secret video recordings, that he, evidently, was involved with various intelligence services, international arms dealing, and that he was in possession of explosive blackmail material against virtually everyone he ever met.

Jeffrey had people murdered and / or intimidated to silence anyone who complained or found out about any of this.

And I never imagined, or at that early stage realized, that "G" coordinated some of the most devastating parts of this living nightmare: the assembly line like recruitment and grooming of likely thousands of young girls to supply her and Jeffrey's twisted sexual escapades and international blackmail machine. Ghislaine, of course, denies all of this.

She is legally, as of this writing, still presumed innocent and has been, at this stage, convicted of no crime.

Those of us who know her or who were victimized by her know better.

We are extremely grateful for the courageous work of the investigators, prosecutors and support staff that made her arrest and prosecution possible.

Outwardly, she was a mega globetrotting socialite. A self-proclaimed patron of saving the oceans, a mere "girlfriend" to serial blackmailing prolific pedophile Jeffrey Epstein.

I distinctly recall her bragging about all the young girls she found and "*broke in*", as she once described it, to satiate her and Jeffrey's perverted sexual desire for children. How she would freely show me numerous videos stunned and terrified me. She would seduce me into threesomes with her and other adult women when I expressed no interest in anything else. When I asked why she was so attentive to Jeffrey's every whim, she said she "loved" him, and as time went by, she, "had no choice." Ghislaine showing me videos of both of them having sex with young girls, using sex toys on them and on each other was disgustingly horrendous beyond description.

At one point, as I attempted to flee, a security guard held a gun on me as Jeffrey tried to threaten me about going to authorities.

Other extreme videos I saw were of exceptionally powerful and famous people. Some now in the news, others not to my knowledge.

Rock star Mick Jagger, former United States President Bill Clinton and his wife, Hillary. Politicians, British Royalty, including several with Prince Andrew with minors, black and white footage of Princess Margaret and the ultra-famous rock star and another man. Australian

33

politicians and celebrity. A Canadian celebrity. A very famous law professor. Various well-known attorneys. Actors Kevin Spacy, John Travolta, a Japanese politician, Harvey Weinstein, modeling agent Jean Luc Bernal, Ghislaine, Ehud Barak and many more.

8 PRISONER IN A MANSION

Incongruous as it may seem, it is a fact that I, while a fugitive, went for assistance, if that was even possible, back to the Palm Beach mansion on El Brillo Way.
The very house I thought I'd never see again.
I met with Ghislaine who said that Jeffrey was out of town.

I quickly explained the situation and told her I needed at least a 100k to leave the area and lay low for a while. I knew they kept that and more in his house from the times he purchased jewelry from me there with immediate accessible large amounts of cash.

She quickly took me to one of the upstairs bedrooms and insisted I lay down with her and then she explained that she would help me immediately if I helped her with an emergency, or "an urgent matter", were her exact words, initially.

Exhausted, she stripped off my clothes and led me to a shower. Quickly undressing she showered with me and

██████████████████████████████████

Back in the bed she brought me a glass of soda. It didn't taste quite right. In bed she was asking for me to murder Jeffrey! She'd give me the 100k if I agreed then and there. I'd agree to anything at this stage just to get my hands on the cash to leave and never look back.

So, after asking her why, given that she was so much in love with him, did she want him dead. She said he was tipped off and knew he was facing imminent and very serious legal trouble and she was afraid that all of the videos of her and the young girls they had sex with would put her in prison for the rest of her life. She remarked that Jeffrey was very dangerous, knew everyone in politics and law enforcement, and that he, "would be the death" of her.

Stunned I asked, "Why ask me?" You have many far more qualified and dangerous people from all over the world who could do it." She was terrified, or so she seemed, and told me, "Yes, but they are far more loyal to him", not to her, and he would kill her first if they mentioned it to him that she wanted him dead.

Because of the very effective façade I portrayed on my own stage at times, also known as Shakespeare's brilliant observation, one of a highly competent man of means and danger, flashing guns and all, I've had others ask me the exact same thing before: To kill people for them.

Incredibly, they *keep a*sking. Including recently when an individual known as "The Godfather of ███████", asked me to murder several people he scammed out of their life savings and that had gone to authorities against him. This guy posed as, "the wealthiest man and only

36

billionaire in ███████████ ."

Asserting that he is personal friends with the incredible humanitarian and rock star, Jon Bon Jovi, country music star Garth Brooks and many others, as well proclaiming that a certain A- list celebrity wanted to hire him, a self-proclaimed decades-long and infamous hitman, to kill another top of his game and Hollywood icon A-list celebrity. And this list goes on.

Ghislaine made it clear that she knew that all she is doing was to find and train a de facto assembly line of underage girls for Jeffrey was illegal and that she was not only recruiting and training them, but she was also clearly engaged in and enjoying sex of every type with them, Jeffrey and others. Even including the use of sex toys, threesomes, and orgies. All secretly filmed at ever changing locations. Her concern during this, our last time together, was her legal exposure. She never once demonstrated an ounce of concern for her many victims or anyone else, unless feigning concern could benefit her, ultimately.

I noticed when I arrived some computers were out of place and there were cables and wires everywhere. Discs and USB drives in plastic bins labeled, and some with women's names on them.

I felt faint and as I believed we were having a threesome again with her adult assistant. I was slipping out of consciousness and told her I would think about it and if she would take the restraints off, we would talk about it. She said that if I didn't agree then and there, she would call the police to the house and turn me in.

As I said, I was a wanted fugitive at this time, so I bluffed and agreed before passing out. Not before telling her that I wanted one million dollars to kill him.

She said, "it's possible", and I drifted off.

Best I can tell I was unconscious about one and a half days, on and off.

A few times I awoke, and I was being sexually abused by Ghislaine as she explained she put Viagra in my drink. When I asked what she put to knock me out she just smiled and told me I shouldn't be concerned about it and not to worry it just helped me rest. As she was abusing me, I struggled to get free to no avail. I was in pain and told her repeatedly to stop. She mostly ignored me continuously doing things to me completely against my will. She ███████████████████████████████████████ ███████████████████████████████████████ ███████████████████████████████████████ █.

When it was over and I was pleading to be released, she made me promise to help her with Jeffrey and threatened to call the police and turn me in if I refused her. Several times she told me she would supply any model I want for a massage or sex or both. I steadfastly refused.

To appease her and try to gather any information I could, I looked at other photos and everyone in them was a very young teenager. These girls were between perhaps 12 and 14 years old. Petrified, I knew I needed to flee and try to get these two arrested to protect their victims.

Once she untied me and gave me some juice, I began to recover and pretended all was fine. I quickly showed and she brought me $5,000.00 in cash and told me she would give me $50,000.00 later that night as a down payment to kill Jeffrey. I convinced her I'd do it just so I could get away from her.

She even had a few horrendous ideas that she suggested would be appropriate including ███████████████████████████████████████ ███████████████████████████████████████ █.

Too gruesome to contemplate. Sarah came in, then left again.

I then noticed bins of discs and USB drives and was hoping they were some of the same types that I was shown. Meaning, containing materials highly incriminating to them. I was determined to slip out with them, and ultimately, I did.

As if the experience with them couldn't get any more bizarre, there was a medical device that was so unusual, Jeffrey was eager to show it in operation. On video someone was using it to almost immediately heal wounds, scars and ███████████████. He said he had some top scientists analyzing it to attempt to reproduce it. To reverse engineer it, he said, because he claimed it came from "aliens" and "a downed UFO that I purchased from ████████".

I have no idea if he was lying about its origins however, I did see it in actual use. He had a smirk on his face when he told me the story of its origin as though he knew I didn't believe it, yet it worked. He certainly had the funds to purchase something like this from any individual or government that originally had it or recovered it from any alleged alien source.

Also, when the small container that it was in was opened, it immediately ████████████ ██████████████████. This alone made it very convincing that it was an authentic alien origin device as he said it is.

Grabbing a pen, I went to the back of a ██████████ I pressed in hard and quickly put my initials, the month and year, because I didn't know the exact date at this stage due to being drugged. And I added the last four digits of my social security number to hopefully one day be able to prove to authorities that I was held essentially hostage

39

there.

There was a trophy I wanted to take, a small, nice model of one of Jeffrey's planes with his initials on it. But I left it behind in the rush to flee with the two bins and the odd medical device.

I laid back as Ghislaine was coming and going from the room. Pretending to doze off, I was dressed and waited for a chance to leave with these bins unnoticed. Then to get off the property with them.

I knew that quickly walking to where I need to get to safely carrying these bins in Palm Beach would be highly suspicious. When I was active as a jewel thief, I learned it was best to be calm, walk or drive confidently and with calm purpose, as if I belonged, and never look back or even side to side.

In an instant my opportunity arrived, and I stacked the relatively small bins and stealthily made my way down the curved staircase.

In the moment, when halfway down, I ran into ██ .

Incredibly it worked, and I received completely unexpected assistance to flee.

Dropping me off, I quickly located other containers for the contents of the bins and just dumped everything into two cardboard boxes and quickly wrote on each one the title and person each was going to as well writing on each, "These contents belong to Jeffrey Epstein and Ghislaine Maxwell El Brillo Way, Palm Beach. Arrest them please." That way I *knew* they would be acted on.

One went to ████████████████ and the other to ████████████████ .

I can only assume they had zero evidentiary value or were

in no way incriminating because I never heard anything about them ever again.

9 EPILOGUE

As of this writing, I have attempted to express many of the experiences that I had during my association with Jeffrey Epstein, Ghislaine Maxwell and a few minor players of their inner circle. This is Book One of a series for a reason.

Ghislaine's federal trial in New York City is currently underway. A trial I certainly try not to follow and simply because it brings back very difficult memories and utter disgust to be reminded of what she did to so many innocent lives.

Though some of the attorneys and professionals say that I too was a victim of sorts I, as a man, have trouble seeing myself that way.

It was my decision to meet these people on their terms to accomplish my ends which at the time, basically served to help feed my cocaine addiction.

Consistently I drew the line when anything to do with a minor or the implication of one came up. Though there was a lot of traffic in and out of the house in Palm Beach, generally speaking, I was routinely told that these were models and or these were women that are doing massages for Jeffrey and Ghislaine.

Much of the artwork inside the house depicted what seemed like very young girls, many nude and in suggestive poses, but again these were deemed "art" by Jeffrey and therefore, not necessarily considered illegal or pornographic according to him at the time. To this day I don't know. I don't know the legal distinctions. All I know is there was a creepy collection in his home and as a general rule, I did not try to spend much time in that house.

I insisted to both Ghislaine, Jeffrey, and other staff to not ever record my name in the visitor's log.

My hope now is that the ever popular and simultaneously treacherous Ghislaine will be convicted in federal court in New York.

If not for all the harm she's done to the young girls she's provided for Jeffrey and had sex with herself, then for at least for the few that were able to bravely press charges and prosecute; sometimes years later.

If anyone reading this would be so callous to think "well it's no big deal because many of them were consenting or paid or had their education or other things paid for by these ultra-wealthy people; Ghislaine and Jeffrey", remember this and that is that under law, any sort of sex with a minor, paid for or not, with any underage of consent person- male or female, is statutory rape.

Far more, just imagine if you had a daughter or any female loved one in your life, your sister, your wife, your mother, your lady friends for example, and imagine at 12 to say 14-years old, they went through this hell. Coming from a background of financial socioeconomic hardship, and in some cases, prior abuse and addiction, then to also cruelly have their innocence and their lifeblood stripped away by these atrocious pedophiles. How would you feel?

Let's continue to support these many victims, the victim advocate attorneys that assist them, and the men and women of law enforcement federal, state, investigators, and prosecutors as they continue to stand up in the face of these most horrible of human beings, that none of us can figure out, yet they literally walk amongst us with an astounding disguise of normalcy. At the same time, they relentlessly victimize the vulnerable at every turn.

The end….. *or is it?*

Gary Greenberg grew up in the Philadelphia area and attended Penn State University, where he mostly studied rugby, beer, and coeds, and miraculously graduated with a B.A. degree in journalism in 1976.

He has now been writing professionally for more than 40 years, primarily as an award-winning newspaper reporter and editor.

Since 1999, he has owned and operated the freelance writing service SuperWriter, Inc. He's also written books, including the crime novel Dead Man's Tale. In 2019, he co-authored with William Steel the riveting true crime memoir *Sex and the Serial Killer: My Bizarre Times with Robert Durst.*

In recent years, Gary has primarily specialized in holistic and alternative medicine. He's written more than 300 published articles in that field as well as the transformative health guide, *The Beer Diet: How to Drink Beer and NOT Gain Weight.* For more information about Gary and his work, go to the-beer-diet.com.

In William Steel's Corner is the Spin Man Himself, **Tom Madden**. Until his golden ship comes in, now well provisioned and clearly under sail, William Steel is more a friend than a PR client right now. Still, my award-winning PR firm TransMedia Group would like nothing more than to publicize his many projects, such as his starring role in a TV series currently in production and his books, including one he wrote while in prison, *Sex and the Serial Killer: My Bizarre Times with Robert Durst.*

Now his latest one is about to break loose about Jeffrey Epstein's purported madam Ghislaine Maxwell, about whom Bill has intimate knowledge just as he had about convicted murderer Robert Durst in an expose for which I gave the subtitle "Dursturbed." But I did promise him, and I will gladly carry out my promise to send out nationally the first news release about his latest venture as I admire this prolific writer's determination to succeed, post-incarceration, this time, lawfully.

Bless him, Bill has truly learned his lesson having served a draconian 18 years in prison for a non-violent offense, where I met him, with me on the outside rooting for him on the inside, and with the assistance of The Ticktin Law Group, helping to secure his release. And this is not "Spin" from the title of my first book *"Spin Man."*

Today, this talented man's bright future includes his desire to bring more social justice and fairness to inmates who, like him, have learned their lesson and are deserving of a second chance. Steel is also keeping up his great, brave work of helping to free wrongfully incarcerated prisoners, while advocating for crime victims.

A word about me is I'm all about words, including my most recent book, my fifth, *Wordshine Man*, due out in early 2022, about how to make words capture attention and provoke actions that accomplish worthy objectives as I intend my blog MaddenMischief.com also to do.

I've been writing all my life, starting as a journalist, then as #2-ranked executive at NBC and now as founder and CEO of TransMedia Group serving clients worldwide since 1981.

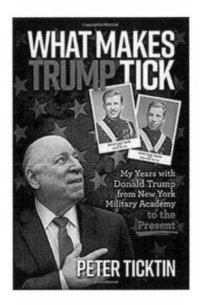

Peter Ticktin, Esquire

When he's not writing books, advocating for victims, speaking at major conferences or running one of the sharpest boutique law firms in the country, *The Ticktin Law Group,* Peter Ticktin is the attorney who helped develop the doctrine of manifest injustice in Florida and is responsible for accomplishing many other firsts in the law while becoming injustices toughest adversary.

He attended New York Military Academy where his commanding officer was none other than **Donald Trump** with whom he developed a lifelong friendship and wrote a book about, "*What Makes Trump Tick.*"

Ticktin first practiced in Ontario, Canada, as a barrister primarily in the criminal courts, arguing numerous appeals, and even changed the law regarding breaking and entering before the Supreme Court of Canada.

When Ticktin began his practice in Florida, the state was wrapped in the anguish of the AIDS epidemic. Ticktin lead the way in redressing wrongs perpetrated on AIDS victims. It was due to Ticktin's efforts that hospitals and physicians changed their procedures to assure HIV test results stayed confidential.

In the years following, Ticktin was on the cutting edge of the law as lead counsel on the only organ donation case to ever get to trial, and he was able to prevail in a two-week CourtTV trial on national television over an organ procurement organization, which harvested the organs of a 7-year-old child who was not brain dead.

Ticktin has tried scores of cases including ones regarding mortgage foreclosure defense, where he has helped in development of the law in not only his own appeals, but by submitting amicus briefs. He unearthed the Robo-signers, and evidence he accumulated was all the Attorney Generals of the 50 States needed to obtain a $30 Billion settlement from the big banks.

For this work and other work and community involvement, the Daily Business Review in South Florida honored Ticktin with a "Distinguished Leader" award in his profession.

William Steel, Author

ABOUT WILLIAM STEEL

In his first gripping memoir, *Sex and the Serial Killer, My Bizarre Times with Robert Durst*, William Steel reveals the depths of the scion's depravity, and he demands justice for Durst's victims and their shattered families.
The book was *Covered on Crime Stories with Nancy Grace and worldwide media*. Available for purchase from WilliamSteelAuthor.com on Amazon, and wherever books are sold.

Contact William Steel directly at:
William@WilliamSteelAuthor.com

William Steel, now a successful author on the rise, has been aptly named, *"THE PREMIER EXPERT IN WRITING TRUE CRIME...THE VOICE OF A GENERATION"*, due in large measure to his engaging, straightforward prose, and his colorful life experiences which have resulted in Steel colliding with many high-profile notorious and diabolical criminals.

In this series of true crime novels, GHISLAINE SENSATIONAL AND IMPURE, the unspeakable is spoken and the truths are no longer hidden. This first book is Ghislaine Maxwell stripped bare.

Readers swiftly become transported into the Mephistophelian criminal underworlds shrouded in veils of opulence, steeping of immeasurable wealth and debauchery in equal measure, spearheaded by Jeffrey Epstein, Ghislaine Maxwell, and their coconspirators.

What used to be a marginally more discreet- *although still publicly known*- inner circle of exploitation and puppeteering by Jeffrey Epstein and Ghislaine Maxwell together, under his direction, has now undergone a drastic shift in power since Epstein's mysterious death.

It has yet to be determined if and how Ghislaine will take over as Epstein's replacement, if she will be convicted, if she will be acquitted and live life under the radar, or if she will remain a public fixture.

With this first book in the series, *GHISLAINE SENSATIONAL AND IMPURE*, a raw, compelling account from Steel's personal insider experiences, more importantly, the reader will gain foundational knowledge helpful for understanding and empathizing with the immeasurable, horrific ongoing suffering and anguish that remains with the many victims of Jeffrey Epstein and Ghislaine

Maxwell, *including William Steel,* who also suffered at the hands of Ms. Maxwell.

Coming soon!
Projects Debuting in the Summer of 2022:

William Steel will light television screens ablaze and *steal* every scene with the debut of the revolutionary docuseries / reality tv program chronicling William Steel's life, post-incarceration, while living amongst a house of weird strangers. The show will be airing on a major network. Stay tuned! *You can't miss it!*

GHISLAINE SENSATIONAL AND IMPURE II
William Steel's second book in the *GHISLAINE* series will focus on the aftermath of Ghislaine Maxwell's criminal trial in New York.

Steel will interview world-renowned experts in the fields of Victimology, Psychology, Criminology, Victims' Rights, and Law.

Steel is leading a progressive, interdisciplinary movement in a quest for effective solutions to what can and should be done to advance advocacy efforts and, ideally, to discover and share successfully strategies for healing to help the victims of Epstein, Maxwell and others like them.

Dr. Mary Bass and William Steel join forces to #FreeDaveReinhardt

Learn about the wrongful conviction case of innocent crime victim David Michael Reinhardt in California and how the Fresno Inheritance Mafia has targeted Dr. Mary Bass for murder for advocating for Dave!
Learn more at: FreeDaveReinhardt.com

Send a letter, a card, or a donation directly to David to show your support: Mr. David M. Reinhardt F-07622 CTF SA 236 P.O. Box 705 Soledad, CA. 93960-0705

APPENDIX

https://www.scribd.com/document/548521437/
Ghislaine-Maxwell-New-York-Sealed-Criminal-Case-
Indictment-Case-1-20-Cr-00330-AJN

https://www.scribd.com/document/548520366/Jeffrey-
Epstein-Police-Report-Palm-Beach-County-Florida-2006

https://www.scribd.com/document/548519775/JE-
Arrest-Warrant-06-9454CF-A99-Palm-Beach-County-
FL-07192006

https://www.scribd.com/document/548520114/Jeffrey-
Epstein-True-Bill-Solicitation-06-9454CF-Palm-Beach-
County-FL-2006

https://www.scribd.com/document/548520493/Jeffrey-
Epstein-Palm-Beach-County-Florida-NPA-Non-
Prosecution-Agreement

https://www.scribd.com/document/548520619/Original-
Jeffrey-Epstein-2019-New-York-Criminal-Case-
Indictment-Case-1-19-Cr-00490-RMB

https://www.scribd.com/document/548520795/Jeffrey-
Epstein-Transcription-New-York-Criminal-Case-Status-
Conference-held-on-July-8-2019-120-p-m

Also available on the author's website at:

WilliamSteelAuthor.com

Made in United States
Orlando, FL
15 May 2022

17875179R10045